A Queens' Guide to Dating the Christian Way

Dating and Staying in the Will of God

TJ Woodard
Alton L. Fitch

A Queens' Guide to Dating the Christian Way: Dating and Staying in
The Will of God
Copyright © 2018 by Tamika Woodard

All rights reserved. No part of this book may be reproduced or transmitted in any form or by any means without written permission from the author.

ISBN-13: 978-0692070635
ISBN – 10: 069207063X
Library of Congress Control Number: 2018901998

Printed in USA

Dedication

To the graduates of Queen Series Class #001 (Jasmine, Courtney, Erica, Jasmyn, Jaenyl, Kelli Ann, Chyna, LeBreeze, Olivia, Donya, Keisha), Minister Claudette and my ladies from Ladies Night In (Nicolette, Schley, Gernae, Lanaiya, Gina, Carlita, Vania, Vernell & Andrae) I dedicate this book to you. After my separation from my husband, God placed it on my heart to start a mentorship program to help young ladies recognize who they are and to encourage them to walk in their true purpose. I thank each of you ladies so much for trusting me to help you along your journey. I am so proud of all of you and all you have and will accomplish. I love you dearly. Know that I also learned from you all.

To my past…thank you!

Table of Contents

Preface

Introduction

God's Not Dead…Neither is Chivalry 2

Diamonds in the Rough 6

The Waiting Game 11

Love or Lust 18

He That Findeth a Wife 21

My Father's Approval 25

The "It" List 27

Dating in the New Age 31

Put a Ring On It 34

Conclusion 41

Acknowledgements 45

About the Authors 49

Preface

Why *A Queens' Guide to Dating the Christian Way*? This book came to fruition after going through a divorce from my second husband. Divorced twice, this was a hard pill for me to swallow, because I did not marry just for it to end in divorce. Before the second divorce was finalized, I was separated for a little over two years. During this time of separation, I NEEDED to figure out what I was doing wrong. I learned so much about myself, including that I did not love myself the way God loved me. Nor did I see myself the way God saw me, and most importantly, I didn't trust God the way I needed to; because if I did, I would have waited on God to send me the man he created specifically for me. It wasn't until I was in my 40's, two divorces later, and after many, many, mistakes that I realized that I didn't need to look for validation from a man and if I had just followed the instructions of the Word of God, I could have saved myself a lot of hurt and pain. But then I wouldn't have had a testimony.

After my divorce, I tried getting back into the dating scene and found how much things had changed. After finding myself and really learning that I am a QUEEN and should be treated as such, dating has been quite a challenge. I learned to put a demand on what I desire and am now patient enough to wait and ensure that what I want is also in alignment with what God wants for me. My desire is to help women of all ages see their true worth and know that if they walk with God, he will give you the desires of your heart.

Introduction

A Queens' Guide to Dating the Christian Way is a book of basic principles that align with what the Bible says about what women should do to prepare for their mates. The Bible gives us specific instructions and if we follow these instructions, we will have successful relationships and marriages. Note, I DID NOT say perfect relationships and marriages but successful ones!

Dating the Christian Way simply means trusting God to send our mates but before then, knowing our value and worth; which will help us make better decisions. The book is intended to be transformational and cause the reader to dig deep and think about past, current and future relationships. It will consist of setting some realistic relationship goals, taking time to "screen" the potential mate to attempt to avoid attaching ourselves to those who won't make the cut, and dating with a purpose.

In this book, you will find some similar things to other self-help books. You may not agree with everything and that's okay. If we can get you to at least think about what we've written and cause you to think before entering another relationship or even evaluating the relationship that you are currently in, then we've done our job.

Chapter One
God's Not Dead...Neither is Chivalry

This chapter means exactly what the title states. We know God is not dead; although we can't see Him, we believe that He lives. Well, I want you to know that chivalry is not dead either, even though I know you may have heard the phrase "Chivalry is Dead" many times before. To be honest with you, chivalry never left, but as women we started to lower our expectations and stopped holding men accountable for treating us like the Queens we are. We stopped demanding or should I say allowing a man to be a man, thus accepting chivalry being "dead."

Miss Independent

When did things change? Well, we often refer to the term "independent woman" when we speak about women who possess the "I don't need a man" attitude. They are the women who have been forced into being independent; meaning that they do not have to depend on a man. Examples of this include single mothers raising children, the career-driven woman, or maybe the idea that women can do what a man does sometimes.

Women, let's not get it twisted. Although Philippians 4:13 says we CAN do all things through Christ and Alicia Keys and Beyoncé have created theme songs like "Superwoman" and "Run the World (Girls)" doesn't mean we have to. I've been guilty of this myself.

Women, it's time we learn how to balance our independence with stepping back and allowing men to do what they were created to do which is provide & protect. There are men out there who would like to open the doors, let you walk through the door first, pull out your chair, pick up the check, but we have taken these acts of chivalry away from them by:

1. Not allowing them to do these things for us.
2. Not expecting them to do these things for us.
3. Not believing we deserve for a man to do these things for us.

Don't get me wrong. There's nothing wrong with feeling like a superwoman or that you run the world, but we have to stop emasculating our men and start empowering them to be men. We were created to be the helper to the man, not to take charge, control, or try to be the man.

Now, before you get in your feelings, we're not taking all the blame. Men have also become lazy. Some men no longer feel the need or believe that they should have to open a car door, pull out a seat, or even help a lady with her coat. Nowadays, you can barely get a man to give up a seat on the train when he sees a lady standing. This is ludicrous. However, as women we really have to start requiring these things of men. We have to start training our young boys and young men to do this for us and for our daughters.

It all starts with knowing our worth. I didn't know my worth, so I accepted all kinds of things from everyone, especially men. Some men would naturally treat me nicely, because of the way I carried myself. Others didn't and that was because:

- When they tried, I would beat them to it. Yes, I was that independent woman that I spoke about.
- They were lazy, and I accepted it. I didn't require anything more.
- When I was most confident with myself it showed.

A friend told me that I should never get out of a car before allowing the man to open the door for me. After years of accepting less, he reminded me that there were real men left in the world and that chivalry was not dead. Let me tell you, once I received this reminder, I was a force to be reckoned with. I like to joke that he created a little monster with that tip. At this point in my life, I can honestly say that some men won't stand a chance. Men who once knew me will not recognize the new me who has now learned her value and her worth.

Of course, I have a dating story. For the sake of privacy, we're going to call this guy RC which stands for Ruth Chris, the place of our first date. Shortly after my divorce was finalized and at the suggestion of one of my girlfriends, I decided to try online dating. I met this guy, we talked for some time and went on our first date. On the way to the date I was going over everything my male friend told me about chivalry and boy was I ready. So here goes:

Strike 1 – I was running a little late due to traffic (men typically expect this of a woman), so I call to let RC know that I would be running 5 – 10 minutes behind. He sounded annoyed, I figured that was setting the tone of how the rest of the date would go. I arrived but since I was unfamiliar with the area, I called to let RC know I was pulling up but wasn't sure where the restaurant was. He told me to drive around because he's sure I would find it. Wait…what?!?! So now I'm annoyed! I thought maybe he would offer to meet me outside or at least stay on the phone to guide me to the location. He did not. Instead, I got myself together, found a park and proceeded to the restaurant.

Strike 2 – I walked toward the restaurant, thinking the guy would meet me at the door, but he was nowhere to be found. I walk in and after briefly looking around, I politely ask the greeter if she seated someone by the name of RC. As I stood waiting for 2-3 minutes, she points to a guy sitting alone and suggests that may be the guy I'm looking for. I looked over and he's sitting down, looking at me while I search for him and he never comes over to greet me. Ok so now I'm thinking, am I being over the top and petty?? The date was comical, but it wasn't as bad as I thought it would be, so I thought I would give him a chance to redeem himself. Sadly, that leads to the third strike.

Strike 3 – Dinner is over, and we leave the restaurant. He asked to walk me to my car. Here we go. Now normally, when I walk, it's fast and I always find myself a few steps ahead. But I've learned that this doesn't give a man the opportunity to take the lead. So, this time, I slowly walk towards my car giving him the opportunity to "make things right" but guess what he does? He stops at the back of my car and says, "Have a good night and get home safely." He did not open my door nor did he make sure I was okay.

I know this story has a little humor to it, but it has a point as well. Now that I know my worth, I know that I deserve certain things. And no, I'm not man bashing or putting RC down. He may be a good guy, and honestly it was more than the three strikes that caused things not to go past the first date, however, knowing how I should be treated as a Queen and a child of the Most High; I just can't settle for anything less.

Ladies, I say all this to say we are royalty and should be treated as such. Our Father God is a King. Maybe you don't want anyone opening your doors, pulling out your chairs and that's okay. But you have to determine what it is that you do want and need because of who you are and Whose you are and know that you don't have to settle for anything less. You also have to be willing to give the same thing that you are expecting of your significant other. You can't expect chivalry when you're not giving respect and taking care of the person you want to be your mate one day.

Chapter Two
Diamonds in The Rough

The first rule to dating is knowing your worth. What this means is, knowing how to love yourself so that you can then know how you want your significant other to love you.

As a woman, I know that we are our worst critics. We tend to be harder on ourselves than anyone else. In order for us to have truly successful relationships, we must first love ourselves the way God created us. Psalm 139:14 says *"I give thanks and praise to you, for I am fearfully and wonderfully made; wonderful are your works, and my soul knows it well."*

We all go through physical changes such as gaining and losing weight, our hair changes, we age and other things too. With that being said, we MUST work to keep our temples holy by working to maintain what God has created. The diamond, jewel, Queen that you are!

Many may not understand the process it takes for a "girls' best friend" to become a diamond. This process is not an easy one. I will explain. If you fully understand how something can go through so much and come out so beautiful, then you will know exactly how God feels about you.

Typically, women like what they call "bling", "carats" or whatever the latest term is now. To be honest, for most of us the goal in dating is to get to the diamond. It may not matter how big or small, but the fact is that we want someone to, as the Beyoncé song says, "put a ring on it."

Well I'd like to share some interesting facts on how a diamond is formed. Maybe then you will understand why as women, we go through so much before recognizing our true beauty but also hopefully you will learn and appreciate your own value. No matter where you are in your life, it is imperative that you understand that you are a beautiful diamond. You're a Queen and worthy to be treated as such.

There are many videos and articles that describe how a diamond is made. I had the opportunity to watch several but the one that stuck out to me the most was a YouTube video by National Geographic and the steps are as follows:

1. Diamonds (Carbon) are formed at the deep earth's mantle where they are super-<u>heated</u> and centered between the crust and the core.
2. <u>Intense pressure</u> then changes the molecular structure of carbon crushing the atoms together.
3. The pressure forces the atoms into a <u>new structure</u>.
4. Under extreme pressure and temperatures that are approximately 2,000 degrees Fahrenheit, the carbon becomes a <u>diamond</u>.

I have underlined some keywords that I want you to think about, especially when comparing who you are to a diamond.

I'm sure I am not the first person who has used this analogy but looking at all that you have been through in your life and comparing it to the process of a diamond being made; I am sure that there are many similarities. I believe God uses a similar process when preparing us for what and who He really has for us.

Where we make the mistake is that we don't wait for God to bless us with who He has for us. I am the first to admit that I have been guilty of this. From my personal experience, it was because I didn't realize my own true value and the person God created me to be. I saw the flaws, where I came from, what I didn't have, the past hurts and mistakes and even what others said about me so much that it took me 40 years to truly love and appreciate every part of who I am; the good, the bad, and the ugly. What I can say now is that I KNOW who I am, I expect nothing but the best because I am worthy of all things great. Now don't get me wrong, I'm not seeking the "perfect" man but I'm patiently waiting for the one God made perfect for me.

Looking back and understanding how diamonds are made, I see how the heated and intense pressure of the situations I have had to endure that led to the crushing and pressing down of my inner being. This has now resulted in me becoming and accepting the beautiful woman I am today. This is the diamond that I am referring to in this chapter. If it had not been from the pressures, the heated situations, feeling bogged down and unworthy of the love that is truly waiting for me I would not have grown to understand who I am and Whose I am.

Now you may ask, what does this all have to do with dating the Christian way? It has a lot to do with it. I can't say this enough, in order for someone to love us the way we deserve to be loved, we must first love ourselves. We must understand how we want to be loved and we only learn that when we recognize the beauty that is within us. Don't get me wrong, the physical appearance is all well and good but what is it worth if your soul is ugly?

When looking at your previous dating experiences conduct an evaluation on who they were and what made you choose them? Then ask yourself, what about them made you believe they were the right person for you. Once you have done this, then ask yourself if knowing what you know now about yourself, your value, your worth…would you choose them again?

I've been married twice. Learning my value and worth doesn't take anything away from my previous marriages because I learned a lot from both of my ex-husbands but also, I wasn't able to truly love them the way they deserved because I didn't know how to fully love myself. I didn't understand the love my Father God has for me or the way He desires for us to love one another. What I mean is that now in my singleness, I have learned to love myself, I don't feel I need to have someone for the sake of not wanting to be alone. I don't have to rush into anything because I know I am truly deserving of the one God has taken His time and molded just for me. I know that if I just wait on Him, my mate will surpass anything I could have imagined.

Seeing ourselves the way God sees us tends to be difficult for us because we look at ourselves and only see our flaws, our mistakes, our hurt and our pain. I'm here to tell you that God looks at our heart. The Lord told Samuel *"Do not consider his appearance or his height for I have rejected him. The Lord does not look at the things people look at. People look at the outward appearance, but the Lord looks at the heart."* First Samuel 16:7

This is true in how we view ourselves, as well as how we view others. When we look at an attractive man, all we see is what's on the outside. Do we know anything about his soul? Does he love God? Does he pray? Do we know if he has goals or visions? This is important because not everything that looks good is good and not everything that is good looks good. We have to be sure that we're not setting ourselves up for failure simply because what we see is not in alignment with what God sees in us, as well as in those we are choosing to date.

Psalm 139:14 is one of my favorite scriptures. "We are fearfully and wonderfully made". God created you in His image and His likeness. This means you are perfect in His sight and well deserving of all things great. Meditating on His word helps us to see and understand all the things He desires for us. I called this chapter "Diamonds in the Rough" because sometimes when we view ourselves we see the mess, the bad choices, and flaws, but we are diamonds that are ready to shine bright for all the world to see. So, take off those layers that hold you back and free yourself to be the best you that you can be. Rise up and be the Queen that you were created to be because you are a child of the KING!

Chapter Three
The Waiting Game

The Waiting Game! Yes, you read it right. This was not the easiest chapter to write but it could not be avoided. First Thessalonians 4:3-6 (AMP) states:

³For this is the will of God, that you be sanctified (separated and set apart from sin): that you abstain and back away from sexual immorality; ⁴that each of you know how to control his own body in holiness and honor (being available for God's purpose and separated from things profane), ⁵not (to be used) in lustful passion, like the Gentiles who do not know God and are ignorant of his will; ⁶and that (in this matter of sexual misconduct) no man shall transgress and defraud his brother because the Lord is the avenger in all these things, just as we have told you before and solemnly warned you.

I didn't say it, but God's Word is the law. If we are to live a life pleasing in the eyes of God, then we must abide by His Word. Now, I'm not in the position to judge anyone because dating as a Christian I have fallen to both lust and fornication before. However, I have also suffered the consequences of my actions. In spite of my mistakes, God blessed me with three beautiful children because He is a forgiving God, His Grace and Mercy has sustained me.

There is the reason God commanded us to restrain from premarital sex. He created sex to be pure and sacred between husband and wife. I've had this conversation many times before and have listened to others discuss this topic. Many questions arise from this commandment regarding sex and intimacy. Some of the questions asked are:

1) What if I wait until I marry, and the sex isn't good?
2) Shouldn't I test drive the car before I purchase it?
3) How do I know we are sexually compatible if we don't have sex?

And the questions could go on and on. I understand. I have had the same questions. However, what I have learned is that doing it my way didn't work out the way I wanted it to, and I believe it is because I didn't follow God's instructions.

Some believe there should be a waiting period of a few weeks or a few months. How well do you actually know a person after a few months? Would you be willing to give them the most precious part of you in such a short period of time? Some aren't so willing to trust people with their personal belongings, such as their children, car, money, etc.- but are quick to give of themselves to a person without knowing who they really are.

Think about this. Is your thinking in line with what the Bible says? First Corinthians 6:18 reads *"Flee sexual immorality. Every sin that a man does is outside the body, but he who commits sexual immorality sin against his own body."* When we enter into premarital sex, the scripture says we sin against our own body. I know that with society and the media everything is sex. The music we listen to, the shows we watch, and even the trendy clothes we wear, have all been saturated with sexual perversion. I get it. I even have heard the phrase "sex sells". But what is it actually selling? I'll tell you what it is selling:

1. Unplanned pregnancies
2. Higher divorce rates
3. Sexually transmitted diseases

I'm not saying sex is bad but sex out of the will of God (premarital) is a sin and we should acknowledge that. It is not too late to repent and abstain.

For many years I thought I had to give up something to get something. I thought my worth was in having a man look at me, tell me I'm pretty, or he loved me. I thought that "having a man", validated who I was. Once I changed my mindset, I learned that I received more when I didn't give in to my flesh. I received more respect, more love, more honesty, more communication and more peace; Peace of knowing I didn't have to worry about what was going on because I was protected. Protected by the peace of knowing that because I am waiting, I don't have to think about what he's doing or not doing. Peace of not wondering if he's going to leave now that we've had sex. I can now rest knowing that when God does a thing, He makes no mistakes. This gives me the confidence that the man He created just for me is fully equipped with all the right things and when we get together it will be well worth the wait.

I believe without a shadow of doubt that God knows what is truly best for us. Jeremiah 10:23 clearly states, *"O Lord, I know the way of man is not in himself; it is not in man who walks to direct his own steps."* So as a Christian, are we to let God rightfully guide us in every way, especially in our weakness? Of course, we should always look to God for spiritual strength so that we may continue to draw close to Him.

Sexual intercourse should only be between a husband and wife. It is one of the most important expressions of love one can give. It helps to repair, build and strengthen a marriage.

It may seem right as a single person to have sex but is it really? The Bible warns us in Proverbs 14:12 *"There is a way that seems right to a man, but in the end it leads to death."* Psalms 119:1 reads, *"Blessed are the undefiled in the way, who walks in the law of the Lord. God will bless us for our faithfulness. He knows our struggles and He will even make a way of escape when we find ourselves in situations that can lead us down the wrong path."*

God does understand that we are all a product of sin and we do fall short of His Glory but that does not excuse us from our moral obligation to Him in this matter. There have been times when I ended up in bed with someone knowing it was not what I wanted and also not where I should have been because of the commitment I made to abstain, but God saved me from my sin and I was able to leave without giving myself up to this person.

The interesting part that helped me recognize God's grace is that I was being made to believe that I was the only one that my guy was dealing with, only to find out that he was in another relationship and I can only assume that he was intimate with the other woman. This was a time where I thanked God that I made it out without giving myself up because I could have opened myself up to all types of feelings, including the feeling of guilt if I had compromised. Because I had abstained, I was able to see the signs and make better decisions through God guiding me because my mind wasn't clouded due to sexual attachment. I was able to end the relationship without feeling like I had lost something. Was I hurt? Yes. Did I feel betrayed? Definitely. Knowing my value as a diamond, allowed me to know it was his loss and not mine.

The pleasure of sex lasts only a short period of time, but the guilt and shame of knowingly breaking God's law can have far reaching ramifications. If sex sells, then what is it that we are actually selling? Have you calculated the cost? Matthew 16:26 says *"What does it profit a man if he shall gain the whole world, and lose his own soul? Or what shall a man give in exchange for his soul?"*

The truth is, some of our actions can lead to disease, unwanted pregnancy, mental anguish, trust issues and low self-esteem. Are men or women even being faithful in relationships these days? With open relationships and other sexual immoralities, you can never be sure, however with abstaining you lower the risks. I'm a living witness that God's grace can sustain.

Sex is a powerful thing, and when shared between two married people, it works wonders, but when it is abused, it can be awful. In dating the Christian Way, you have to be clear as to how you want to live your life. Once you have made the decision to remain abstinent you have to understand that the enemy will try to test you. Temptations will be stronger than ever. When it comes to dating, you want to establish where you stand simply because dating has changed and nowadays terms such as "Netflix and Chill" have a different meaning.

As Christian daters who have made the decision to abstain from premarital sex, we have to be cautious not to put ourselves in situations where we can risk compromising our belief. I've learned this the hard way as I've tried to get back into dating. What can seem like an innocent act of spending the night together can lead to something more.

I went on a date that was going very well. The guy asked if I wanted to go to my place or his to watch a movie. Something dropped in my spirit that said this probably wasn't a good idea, but I went anyway. I knew I was strong enough to hold out because I knew that my intentions were pure. What I didn't know, was that my date had other plans. In dating, we become comfortable feeling we have self-control but what we cannot do is assume that of the other person.

So back to my story. As the movie came to an end, I was offered the opportunity to stay, since it was late. I was thinking I could crash on the couch however, my date came out of the bedroom butt naked and ready to Get. It. On. Needless to say, it made for an uncomfortable end to the night after I had to let him know that it was not going down.

I learned a valuable lesson that night. I learned that I should never put myself in a compromising position because a situation like that could have gone completely wrong. I also learned that I can't be naïve to think that men, when given the opportunity will not have sex as sometimes it is one of the first things on their mind. Although I knew sex wasn't the intent for me, I was so off the mark to assume that it was the same for him. Ladies, once you have made the commitment to celibacy your decisions must align with what the Word says and how you are choosing to live your life.

One way to prevent any misunderstanding about premarital sex is to be open and honest. Having dialogue is important so that there are no hurt feelings. The worldly view on sex will never be in-line with the Christian view so when dating it is so imperative to find a person who has the same mindset as yours. They should be committed to walking the same abstinence walk as you. Yes, it is extremely difficult nowadays to find people who believe and stand firm in their belief on premarital sex but that is where our faith in God and what He wants for us comes into play. I know we addressed some very important questions earlier on and they are legitimate.

God knows what is truly best for us, and if we put complete faith in Him, He will provide us with the perfect person to fulfill our sexual needs. If we go out and "sample the platter" so to speak, then we show a complete lack of faith and wisdom on our part. If we give up everything before the marriage, then we have nothing left to look forward to. The Honeymoon really isn't a honeymoon because it doesn't feel differently from the days, weeks, or months prior to the marriage. What has really changed except a title?

Again, we are not here to become anyone's moral authority or condemn those for some of the choices they may have made in the past. We all have fallen short of the glory of God, so don't beat yourself up if you fail; but the whole point is to continue to try. For my Queens who ask, "is it too late to abstain even if you are currently in relationships", the answer is no. Pray and ask for forgiveness, make your commitment to God, try your best not to place yourself in that situation again and move on. In addition, have an accountability partner. Let someone close to you know of your commitment. Walk this walk with your partner or a friend. Lift each other up and encourage one another. Know this, if you're currently in a relationship where sex is involved and you make the choice to abstain, the person for you will want to take this walk with you. Pray about it and ask God to help you.

Chapter Four
Love or Lust

Love is an intense emotional feeling towards another person. It's a strong connection that is often times an unbreakable bond. However, lust is a strong desire for someone sexually, usually based upon ones' physical appearance.

Personally, I don't believe any relationship can be built on sheer lust, other ingredients must be involved other than physical attraction.

Over the years our bodies grow old, we become gray, wrinkled and less attractive. If our relationship is built on a quicksand foundation such as lust, then we are left with absolutely nothing.

Lust can often leave us with emotional deficits and feelings of emptiness. This could lead to the dulling of our ability to build a meaningful relationship.

Lust has its place, but only in conjunction with love. There is no greater feeling than being truly loved or in love. Love encompasses all things. It can range from affection to emotional attachment to compassion. Once we find that special person, our love is to be given and accepted unconditionally. When we love someone, we have a feeling of being complete. True love doesn't fade away with time, it only grows.

Like most other things love must be nurtured, watered, fed, and then it can be harvested. When you love someone, you want to spend quality time together other than having sex. Time seems to stand still when you are together. We often become emotionally invested in our mates' well-being. Love has strong core principles such as compassion, forgiveness, tolerance, understanding, openness and protection.

We gave you our personal thoughts on how we felt about love and lust, now let's see what the Bible has to say. Matthew 5:28 says, *"But I say to you, that whosoever looketh on a woman to lust after her hath committed adultery with her already in his heart."* What this means is that when we look at someone desiring to have sex or be intimate with that person we have already sinned as if we have completed the act.

David let his lust get the better of him as described in Second Samuel 11:2. He got up one morning from a nights' sleep and went outside his palace onto his roof and there he saw a beautiful woman bathing. What he should have done was turn away and go back inside, but he didn't, instead he sat there and continued to gaze upon her naked body. So, he lusted after her in his heart and this lead to the murder of Bathsheba's husband, Uriah. We are not saying that lust will lead to you going to such extreme measures, but it can lead to other unwanted and unnecessary consequences of sin, especially if we continue to water and feed our lustful thoughts. As believers, we have to be careful of how we think so that we don't go down that path.

The Bible has so much to say about love; for instance, in First Corinthians 13:4-5 states *"Love is patient and kind, it does not envy or boast, it is not proud. It does not dishonor, it is not self-seeking, it is not easily angered, it keeps no record of hurt."* Imagine if God kept a journal of all the hurt we caused Him and held it against us as we sometimes do to our loved ones, we would all be in trouble.

Ephesians 5:25 states *"For husbands, this means love your wives, just as Christ loved the church."* He gave up his life for us all and this is the type of love the scripture speaks of when instructing husbands on how they should love their wives.

Genesis 2:24 states *"Therefore a man shall leave his father and mother and hold fast to his wife and they shall become one flesh."* This doesn't mean that husbands shouldn't love their parents but in marriage, you have now become one. So, if we follow Biblical principle, we will gain a lot from it and it tells us exactly how we are to love.

Romans 12:10 states *"Be devoted to one another in love, Honor one another above yourselves."* This is one of my personal favorites because it is very short and to the point, if we honor the other person above ourselves, it shows the same unselfish love that God has for us. We should be able to do this with our significant other without fear of being taken advantage of. Christ did the same for us, so it is only right we do the same by following the instructions given to us in His Word.

I believe we are scared to give our all to a person because deep down inside we are afraid to show that kind of love and devotion. This can be because of past hurt in previous relationships. Maybe we are afraid it won't be reciprocated. Whatever the reason, that's not how we are to be, and we have to be careful not to rush into anything. This is where our faith comes in and trusting in the process of letting God send us the mate He has for us we can then let things happen organically.

Chapter Five
He That Findeth a Wife

Proverbs 18:22 (KJV) says *"Whoso findeth a wife findeth a good thing, and obtaineth favour of the Lord."* I'd like to reiterate this scripture. He meaning the man, that finds a wife finds a good thing AND obtains favour of the Lord.

First of all ladies, we have to know and understand our worth. We have to know and understand that WE are the good thing that God is talking about. We have to know and understand that we are the prize and that God has prepared a man who is created just for us. He was created to find us. His good thing. His wife.

I know some women will challenge this by saying "I should be able to go after what I want" or "I'm tired of waiting for him to find me." I get it. Really, I do. But when you don't wait on God and for the person he has for you, you subject yourself to getting the wrong thing or settling for less than what God had designed just for you and believe me you can end up unhappy or even going through what you may not have had to go through otherwise.

Now don't get me wrong, because of God's grace and mercy and because He is a forgiving God He can certainly bless us even after we go ahead of Him. We must repent and ask for His forgiveness, but we must also stay prayed up in our marriages and be willing to fight against the enemies' attacks.

However, waiting and preparing yourself for the husband you desire gives us time for God to work on us preparing us for who He has for us and time for God to complete His work in our companion. If you are giving yourself up to other men, not understanding your role as a wife, and making the common mistakes that we tend to make during the waiting process, then we are going against the will of God and setting ourselves up for whatever consequence that comes with our disobedience.

Did I mention I've been married twice? Yes, I still desire to be married again but this time I have to know without a shadow of a doubt that HE is the one God sent for me. I'm standing and I'm waiting. This makes it easier for me to ward off the ones who are coming at me who I know do not qualify. Settling is not an option. The way I see it, why risk having to do this more than once when you can marry one time and do it the way God intended for us to do it.

Try this exercise. Visualize one thing you have always desired for yourself. It can be a car, a house, a piece of jewelry but think of one thing. Now picture yourself going shopping and purchasing this thing. Next see yourself going home and the very thing you purchased was there waiting for you, but it was bigger and better than what you could have even imagined. Let's say it was a house you thought about but all you visualized was the house.

You never imagined the furnishings, the cars in the driveway, your family that would fill it, you only saw the house. Well that's the difference in how we see things and how God sees things. We only see a portion. Sometimes what we see is not even in God's plan because we see what we want, and He sees what His desires are for us.

Well this is the same for Christian dating. God sees the bigger picture and only wants HIS best for us even in our relationships. How great would that be if you were to wait on God and the man He created to find you was more than you could have ever imagined. As our Father, we are precious to Him and because He created us, only He knows who is deserving of us. No matter our faults and what we've been through we are well deserving of His best. Two marriages later, even I am deserving and will continue to wait on His best.

Now for my Queens who are currently in relationships and ask is it too late for them? The answer is no. God is a forgiving God. You can evaluate the relationship you're in and if it is not in alignment with God's Word then you can repent and begin to change your situation and make a commitment to God that you choose to wait on Him. Pray for strength and discernment. If God instructs you to move, then do so. If you feel that you shouldn't then pray and ask God to work on you and the person you believe is for you because only God can change a person, not us.

What does it mean to be a good wife? And for my men reading this book what does it mean to you to find a good wife? If you have someone--do you truly appreciate her or him or do you take them for granted? Ladies, are you willing to do what it takes to be a good wife? Its human nature to sometimes take for granted the "Good Thing" that God has provided to us, but we have to be careful not to do so.

To me, a good wife is someone that is selfless and devoted to God and her family. She knows that when she puts God first in everything that she does then God will reward her with the spouse and family she so desires.

Proverbs 31 beginning with verse 10 talks about the virtuous woman (wife). This woman is the woman of all women. She's what they call a BOSS! Have you studied what this scripture says about the Godly virtuous wife? Do you fit the characteristics of the virtuous woman? Let's look at a few verses from the amplified version of the Bible says:

Verse 10 - *"An excellent woman (one who is spiritual, capable, intelligent, and virtuous), who is he who can find her? Her value is more precious than jewels and her worth is far above rubies and pearls."* (Yes, this is you, the person reading this book)

Verse 11 – *"The heart of her husband trust in her (with secure, confidence), and he will have no lack of gain."*

Verse 12 – *"She comforts, encourages, and does him only good and not evil all the days of her life."*

The description of the virtuous woman begins at Proverbs 31 verse 10 and ends at verse 31. Read this word. Meditate on it. Understand all that the Word is saying about the virtuous woman so you can be certain that you will be a virtuous wife. In your waiting season and while God is preparing your mate, this is the time for God to work on you and for you to align yourself with Gods' Word as to the type of wife He created you to be. Again, we are not perfect by any means but while we are consulting with friends and imitating relationships we see on social media, reality shows, and through the people we see around us, we should instead be consulting with the Word of God. Everything we need is there. Focus on this and let God do the rest.

Chapter Six
My Fathers' Approval

Traditionally when a guy is interested in dating a girl, to show his respect, he would ask the father for permission to date his daughter. There was a time when a man would have to give something called a dowry, such as goats, jewels, money, or basically something of value to the father in order to marry his daughter. This same idea should remain true now.

God has already chosen the person who is to be "the one." He knows who he is because he created him. Once the "guy" believes in his heart that he is the one, he should be required to ask for your father's approval. I'm not referring to your physical father but your spiritual father.

The man who meets you and believes he is the one God has chosen to be with you and vice versa, needs to seek approval from your Father God. Since this guy is a believer, then he knows what this means. For those who may not understand where I am going with this, I am referring to prayer. The man as well as you, should go to God in prayer asking for wisdom and guidance ensuring that you and your Father God are on the same page.

Some of this may seem repetitive but it really is that simple. When we trust God and operate in His will we minimize the heartache and pain we subject ourselves to when we don't. Seeking God's approval requires several things.

1. Trust in God
2. Faith to believe what He (His Word) says

3. Obedience to follow His Will
4. Praying continuously and walking in fellowship with Him

In reality, as daughters we tend to seek our fathers' approval even when they are not around. That is why we sometimes tend to choose certain types of men because we are looking for that validation or that need for a father figure in the men we choose to date. This is the reason why having our Heavenly Father's approval is imperative to the future of our relationships.

Chapter Seven
The "It" List (Needs vs. Wants)

In any relationship we have **needs** and **wants**, often we confuse the two. This is not necessarily selfish but if not recognized it can lead to the appearance of selfishness and we all know perception is reality.

The word **want** as defined by the dictionary is to fill a need or desire or to wish for. **Needs** as described by the dictionary is a requirement, necessary duty or obligation. So with all that being said what are some of our **needs** and **wants**?

Let's start with our needs because that is the core basis for any relationship. What is it you actually need from your relationship in order for it to be really successful? Is it respect, and honesty? Is it finding someone that shares the same core values as yourself such as religious beliefs and the family hierarchy? Do you believe that the husband is the head of the family? What is the role of the wife and what is the role of the children?

What are your views on finances, making family decisions? Do they save or do they spend frivolously? Are their views in alignment with yours? What are their future goals?

How many children do you want, if any? These are important questions, especially when children are involved. You may end up dating someone who really isn't into children, which may become a problem if they are not accepting of your children. You may not want more children and they do or vice versa. How do you feel about discipline? Who's the disciplinary? This is important in what you would "need" in a person.

We all have emotional needs. Are you the type of person that requires constant attention and reassurance? This is not a sign of insecurity, it is recognizing what is essential for your well-being.

What are your wants? Recognizing them is something that helps determine what you desire in your relationship to be satisfied.

Are you being unrealistic in some of your expectations? If it's something you wouldn't ask of yourself then yes, it may be unrealistic.

Do you have a taste for the finer things in life but are unwilling to make the adjustments required to obtain them? Unfortunately, that's a want and not a need.

Are some of the things we ask for going to be a detriment to any relationship? If so, then it's more than likely a want and not a need.

We all have our wants and our needs, but it is very important to understand the difference between the two. If not recognized, we can derail our relationship.

When we say wants versus needs, this is where you really want to go to work. Sometimes the things we "want" in a relationship can be very superficial. Again, there's nothing wrong with certain things in a person but you have to ask if you are being realistic in your expectations. Do you need a man making a 6-figure income or do you want a man making a 6-figure income? Do you even know what you need or want in a relationship or in a man? As women I know we pray and ask God to send us the man of our dreams but are we being specific about our desires. Are we being specific and realistic in our requests?

Here's another assignment. I want you to make a list specifically outlining characteristics you need in a mate and then characteristics you want in a mate. Really take some time and think about what your desires are. Imagine the person who you believe would truly make you happy and what this looks and feels like. Your list should look something like this:

Needs
God-fearing
Prayer warrior
Supportive
Great communicator
Has a career
Loves family/children

Wants
6'2
Have a high paying job/ nice car
Good hair
Own place
Likes to travel

This is just an example. Your list will be different and should be very detailed. Now this list should be visited quite frequently because as you change, what you seek in a mate may change and some things may shift up and down on your list.

Having this list will help you make better choices when dating because it will help us determine the things that we will not compromise on. Those things should be on the top of the list. It's ok to have this list handy while we are considering who we should date. This should become a permanent part of the dating process. If you are dating now or currently in a relationship, you can do this as well.

Once your list is created, give this list to God. Pray on it. Ask God to take your list and to align your it with His plan for you and trust God to send that person to you.

I joke with my friends because as a military recruiter, we had what we called a prequalifying or pre-screen worksheet. The purpose of this worksheet was to ask specific questions that we knew would immediately disqualify a person from joining. This questionnaire most times would come before meeting with the applicant to avoid wasting the applicants time and the recruiter's time. This prevented us from scheduling appointments with those who we knew did not qualify. I told my girlfriends that I have adopted the same technique to my dating process. Believe it or not they have been waiting for my pre-screen method, so they can do the same. We laugh and joke about it but having this process in place would help to quickly weed out those who are not deserving of our time.

I've been on several dates in the last couple of months. Some have cut me off and some I decided not to pursue. I must say I don't feel bad in the least because everything I have mentioned throughout this book has helped me realize that it's ok and if I wait on God He is going to truly bless me. He knows what I want but more importantly He has already created the perfect person for me. Yes, I missed the mark a few times but I'm still in it to win it and this time I'm coming out on top. Dating isn't easy but when you trust God and love yourself even in your singleness, you will have peace knowing that Mr. Right will soon grace your presence.

Chapter Eight
Dating in the New Age

We believe people have gotten away from the traditional methods of dating and courting one another. In modern day society it is acceptable to date the "New Age style." Match, Facebook, Zoosk, Tinder and other social media outlets have dulled our expectations of one another. Nowadays all you have to do is swipe left or right to find someone. We look for convenience in dating and we shouldn't. I understand the reason behind it though; I even tried it myself. What happens is people can create an idea of themselves and you really don't know who you're getting.

Dating is meant to be a thorough process in which we use to vet our perspective mate. It should be done in person, not strictly through emails, text, social media and other convenient but non-personable methods. My suggestion is if you're going to connect with someone online still keep in mind those things I've said especially pray about it and then work through the dating process of getting to know the person. When done properly, we get the wonderful experience of truly finding what it is we seek from the dating process and one another.

Just think of how much fun it is to actually sit down in front of a person and not a computer screen to talk. You get to feel someone out better when you start to ask questions and see their responses, facial expressions, body language and if they are actually being attentive to your words. When most of the conversation is done over text or computer you don't get to have that valuable experience.

The first date should be fun and in a comfortable setting. It can be something as simple as a nice long walk or meeting for brunch. Have a list of questions you wouldn't mind asking in your head. Don't get to the date and then pull out a long sheet of paper and start grilling the man like a Drill Instructor. TRUST ME that will be the last date from him! How do I know? Well, enough about me, let's get to some of these great talking points, shall we? Like I said before, you don't want to come off like you are being nosey or too inquisitive but take time to feel him out.

1. How do you feel about dating? Are you a casual dater?
2. What are your hobbies?
3. Do you like to travel and if so where have you been?
4. Are you a music lover? (Follow up question) Do you like live music?
5. What is your occupation? Always ask if they like their job, (this invites more conversation).

These are just a few.

Times have changed and I'm not putting down the idea of dating the new age way, however we have lost the importance of human connection and how to effectively communicate with one another. Online dating has its pros and cons. I've personally seen it work for people I know, and it has worked for many others because at the end of the day a relationship is what you put into it. You must ask yourself a question, what are you putting into it if all you are doing is dating via text messages and emails? Would you honestly feel like you are truly getting to know someone? Getting out and actually engaging in conversation and spending time in each other's presence is how you begin to get to know someone.

As we spoke of earlier, that connection is what you want to feel from a person when you're sitting face to face. Things like eye-contact and body language can help you read people. Whether meeting people the traditional way or meeting them on dating websites you can fall victim to meeting a false representative of the person you see, and this can happen whether you meet online or offline. You have to be careful when meeting people on the Internet because of "catfishing" where a person uses someone else's photo as a major false representative of who they are.

I've been "catfished" before actually. I spent time getting to know a person by phone before meeting and thought I had made a real connection. However, when we met the person did not look like his profile, nor the pictures he sent to me directly. Not that it was about his physical appearance but that if he was misleading about his appearance what else would he be hiding. People can write whatever they want when they are creating an online profile. They can build themselves up to be whoever they want to be. They can even play this role for some time. BUT if you take your time and fully get to know the person the real person will eventually present themselves. A person can only fake for so long.

So again, I'm not knocking the new-age way of meeting, but you have to incorporate the traditional ways of dating to ensure this person is the one God has sent to you and not who you are choosing for yourself. I do understand online dating has made life easier for those with busy schedules, the shy person, or the person who likes to have a variety of choices but we cannot forget old-school courtship and communication.

In this day of instant gratification keep in mind that some things take time. I like to compare online dating to a microwave meal. It's cheap, fast and sometimes it can actually be gratifying; but do you know what's really in it? All kinds of artificial ingredients, there may be some real meat but how much?? Now when you date the traditional way, you actually shop for the right ingredients; taking your time to properly prepare and cook your meal. Once it's done you get to sit down at the dinner table and enjoy all of your hard work. The microwave meal can be fine but that homemade meal is so much better.

Chapter Nine
Put A Ring on It

The end goal in dating is to get the ring. We have to be careful not to want the ring so bad that we lose sight of taking time to get to know someone. Sometimes we chase the ring and sacrifice our morals and beliefs only to find ourselves stuck and miserable in a relationship or wanting to get out of one.

Yes, I have another story. I know...I know but here goes. Once I dated a very nice guy I thought I could see a future with. The problem was that he wanted marriage so badly that he didn't want to wait or even consider how I felt. He was ready to marry after knowing me for just a short time. Make no mistake about it, at the time I was desiring marriage and maybe would have even considered marrying him had he taken things slow and wanted to actually get to know me and allow me to do the same. NO! That was not the case at all. While out to dinner one night...he did it. He pulled out a ring and popped the question! Wait...we had only been dating for a couple of months AND how in the world did he find a ring that fast? He was ready, and I went running!

Pause...now I know some maybe asking what's the problem with that. The problem is that he didn't know me and I didn't know him enough to commit to marrying him. He was not in love with me but in love with the desire of being married. He wanted a wife. Women we tend to make this mistake quite often feeling like we're up against our biological clocks or that we're running out of time. Getting the ring is not just about a "rock" or an accessory for that particular finger but it is actually a covenant. A commitment. God honors marriage. That's why it is important that we choose wisely.

Marriage is easy to get into but can come at a great cost when getting out of it. Not just financially but emotionally as well. It not only affects you but the people who are close to you and your significant others. Children, In-laws, Friends are all affected when a relationship ends. This is why what you do in the dating process is so important.

The wonderful process of dating is to determine if you and your potential mate are compatible for marriage. After a year of courting one another you have a general idea if this person is someone with whom you want to "put a ring on it" and spend the rest of your life with.

Some of the questions you need to consider are listed below.

Do you share the same value system and have similar goals in life? Nothing is more strenuous on a marriage than being unequally yoked. So, you should have similar values. This is key and should be discussed early in the dating process. If you don't share the same values, then why waste your time. Bulging arms, a beautiful smile and a big bank account will not help you if his beliefs and values are different from yours. You also want to know if he has goals and what are they?

If your goal is to start a business and conquer the world but his goal is opposite, or better yet he doesn't have a goal or may not agree with your goal, this could cause conflict in the future. You may be a thrifty shopper who likes to budget and shops with thought and a purpose when he may be a frivolous spender and living life as it comes. Amos 3:3 (KJV) *"Can two walk together, except they be agreed."* If you're not in agreement with the important things that are foundational in a relationship then you're setting yourself up for problems down the road; problems that can create bitterness, resentment, anger and more. You may try to deal or even internalize it to make the other person happy but is it worth it in the end? We are talking about having strong, long lasting, God-centered marriages and we want to start now by changing our self-destructive patterns of behavior.

Do you make each other a priority? Your number one goal is to make each other feel like a King and Queen; everything else comes second. Your relationship is like a partnership, never taking the other for granted and making decisions with one another; you should consult with one another no matter how big or small a matter may be.

Sometimes we get so complacent that we forget that we need to continuously "court" or "date" one another. Wow! How many have been guilty of this? You can put me to the head of the line. I'm sorry, but "Netflix and Chill" is not a date. Find someone that you have similar interests but also some differences. Use the differences as an opportunity to learn something from one another. Ladies it's ok to play video games, watch sports, and do something that he likes to do.

DO NOT put your work or your girlfriends before your man! Again, we are dating with a purpose so if the purpose is marriage then remember practice makes perfect. Because we are taking our time waiting for the man God has for us, then he will be well worth all the good things you have to offer. If there comes a time when you're feeling a little neglected it is ok to communicate that to him. Not by nagging him but you could plan a spontaneous date pulling him away from a heavy workload and then let him know you miss him and the time you spend with one another.

Learn to disconnect from social media, girlfriends, work, and any other distractions that doesn't allow you to make your man a priority in your life after God.

Do you often find yourself making long term plans together? If so you're on the right track with someone you want to build a future with. The way to determine the direction your relationship is going is if your "guy" begins to reference future or long-term plans with you in it. It doesn't have to take years for this to happen. If you're dating the person you would want to have a future with then within the first 6 months you should know if you are both on the same page.

Do you accept each other's flaws? Do you accept someone's flaws and still feel like you have found that precious jewel? If you feel you have, then congratulations. I hate to break it to you ladies but there is no such thing as a perfect man. I know this because I spent years looking for him. I let good men go because I thought the next one would have it all and boy was I wrong. The next one came with very different or even more problems than the last one had. I would think maybe I should have stayed with what I had because the new thing…whoa!

My point is that everyone comes with something. You have to give it time because everything looks good in the "honeymoon" stage but when the blinders wear off and after you've had your first argument is when things get real! The same "flaws" you overlook, or think are cute in the beginning turn out to be not-so-cute later down the line.

When dating with the intent to marry, you must consider the fact that you will be accepting this person just as they are. Yes we are constantly growing and developing but the core of a person doesn't change without God. So, take your time and really explore the person you are looking at. Invest time into really getting to know this person to see if you can truly see yourself with him "until death do you part."

Is he or she humble and modest or boastful and full of false pride? You have to be humble and modest in all that you do and that includes relationships. False pride and a boastful attitude has no place in a relationship.

Do they have a forgiving spirit? A forgiving spirit is a must in any relationship. We are going to offend one another at some point in the relationship, so forgiveness is a requirement, it is a command. In order to receive forgiveness, we must be able to truly forgive those whom we have transgressed. Through the shed blood of Jesus Christ, we are forgiven so we must do the same. Matthew 6:15 reads, *"But if you do not forgive others for their trespasses neither will your father forgive your trespasses."*

In relationships and marriage you will practice forgiving and asking for forgiveness. Why? Because we are human and we make mistakes. However, forgiveness has to happen in order for a relationship to work. Forgiveness does not mean bringing up one's mistake every chance you get but it means letting go and moving on. You want to grant the same mercy you would want extended to you when you mess up.

Do you pay each other compliments? A small compliment such as "you make me so happy" means a lot to the other person, so never be afraid to hand out compliments. A compliment goes a long way. Just like we like to receive compliments men like to receive them as well.

There's a book called The Five Love Languages written by author Gary Chapman. This is a MUST for ANY and ALL relationships. If you don't know how you want to be loved, then how can you expect someone else to know. Knowing your love language will help you communicate that to your significant other. Yes, men and women like compliments, recognition, to know they are being appreciated but not everyone wants it verbally. Words don't mean much to some people because they may have received broken promises before. Some people don't like to receive flowers but knowing each other's love languages will ensure effective compliments. Other tests include temperament test and The Four Lenses Assessment that help you better understand others and how we communicate with one another.

Do you love each other's company but still give one another space without feeling slighted? I know we all love our mates but sometimes we need our personal space. There's nothing wrong with that; we all need to take a minute to ourselves just to freshen the battery or to reflect. Now what we can't be is too demanding or smothering. Everyone needs time to themselves or to hang out with friends and/or family or just a reasonable time apart. This gives you time to miss each other and is healthy for relationships. In this instance balance is key.

Do you see positive changes in that person? If so that means that person is willing to evolve. Evolving is a must in any relationship because nothing stays the same.

Do you do things for each other and not expect anything in return? That's a sure sign of a person who cares about you. A person that is willing to give for no reason other than their love for you, is also a person that is willing to go the extra mile to make a relationship work to its fullest.

Do you get along with each other's families? We all know that family is important and to be able to get along with each other's families is a blessing. There's nothing worse than bringing your significant other around and no one seems to care about that person. This will begin to make you as well as your significant other uncomfortable. Discuss family a lot during the dating process. This alone can tell you a lot about a person and whether you two have the same values, goals, and visions when it comes to having or uniting your own families. Find out about the ex-spouse, and the children's parents if there are children from previous relationships.

You want to be with someone you will feel comfortable bringing your family, friends and children around and vice versa. Also communicate with your family as well. I know my family did not always agree with who I chose in my relationships but I never knew it because they only showed love. You want your family to respect your relationship even if they don't agree. When people love you they want what's best for you. However, sometimes they see things we don't so take heed and move forward wisely. Remember to pray about everything and you can't go wrong.

Can you sit down with this person and have a meaningful conversation? Can this person stimulate your mind? Good conversation can lead to a lot of good years together. Communication is key! I will say that again. Communication is key! When the sex is gone and the kids are gone, you will HAVE to talk to each other. Women we have to learn to talk about things other than our girlfriends' drama. The Internet has made it easy. You can Google Search questions to ask to get to know someone. There are dating self-help books and books on anything and everything. Talk about God. You can never run out of things to talk about in the Bible. Explore. Broaden your minds. If you're not doing this already then please start now. Ensure that the person you're dating is mentally stimulating you as well.

These are just a few simple questions you can ask yourself to see if this person is truly the one you want to spend the rest of your life with. If they are answered correctly then by all means, let them "put a ring on it."

Chapter Ten
Conclusion

The scripture says *"we perish for the lack of knowledge"* (Hosea 4:6 KJV) and so I know we've said a lot in the last nine chapters. The goal here is to help. I've made a lot of mistakes. Out of those mistakes came my three beautiful children and now I am here sharing a snippet of my experiences and things I've learned so you don't have to learn the way that I did. Divorce isn't fun. It doesn't just affect the married couple, but it affects the children, the families, and the friends. You can have love and marriage after divorce if you desire it. However, you have to avoid making the same mistakes repeatedly. Take your time. Move cautiously, fully understanding that what God has in store for you is truly worth waiting for. Do your part and work on you. Prepare for your potential mate. Be ready when God sends him to find you.

I hear so many women say they are over dating or that dating is exhausting. To be honest, it doesn't have to be. We make it much harder than it has to be, simply because in the world of instant gratification we want things now and that's not how it works when it comes to the person we are choosing to spend the rest of our lives with.

We leave God out of the equation and think that we know what we are doing and can do it on our own; but we can't. We settle due to low self-esteem or for the sake of not wanting to be alone. We turn a blind eye to things that we should run from. Then we wonder why we end up single, divorced, or hurt. That is not how God intended for relationships to be. Relationships should be beautiful. Marriage was made to last forever; until death do you part. It starts with what we are doing before the marriage. What we are doing in the dating process.

Just like I said in "My Father's Approval", we need someone else to see the things in people we don't see because we're googly eyed and seeing stars, hearts, and butterflies. We need our Heavenly Fathers' wisdom and guidance. We can't think for one minute that in a matter of days, weeks, or even months that we are going to know all that we need to know about a person well enough to take that next step towards walking down the aisle.

There's a process. If it were not so, then God would not have left specific instructions for us when it comes to the person we should date or even marry. I apologize if I'm being repetitive, but I can't seem to say it enough. We must know who we are before we can be any good to anyone else. During your single season, take time to love you. Get to know you. Find and develop your purpose. You have so much within you and the time is now. While you're in your singleness be the best version of you. Pray for your potential mate. Speak words of affirmations and pray to God that your desires be in alignment with His.

Previously quoted, and one of my favorite scriptures states *"I will praise thee; for I am fearfully and wonderfully made: marvelous are thy works; and that my soul knoweth right well"* (Psalm 139:14, KJV) Say this to yourself daily for you ARE fearfully and wonderfully made! Once you realize that you are worthy of all good things you can then require these things from your potential mate.

Our Heavenly Father just like our natural father wants to be involved in our dating process. The same way a natural father has an idea of who he wants for his daughter is the same way our Heavenly Father feels, except He knows EXACTLY who He wants for us because He created him. We have to learn not to move ahead of God and to seek guidance from Him before connecting to those who are not for us.

Second Corinthians 6:14 talks about being unequally yoked with those who are unbelievers and do not share the same values and beliefs.

This can be detrimental to your relationship because although it may not seem like a problem in the beginning, it can surely be one further down the road. This doesn't just pertain to your spiritual walk but when it comes to your views on things like finances, disciplining children, how you handle conflict in the relationship and even sex. Do not take this lightly!

Sex is a big one! Your body is your temple. First Corinthians 6:18 says flee from sexual immorality meaning premarital sex and any form of sexually immoral acts. The Bible says that you sin against your own body. God is a forgiver of sins and again, it's not too late to get on the right track. When you have sex, you become one with that person. It is displeasing to God when you join yourself with the wrong person. It can also cloud your judgement and cause you not to truly see the person for who they really are. Waiting to have sex is not only a command given by God but it is the best thing especially when it comes to diseases, emotional ties, and the idea of giving up the most precious part of you to someone other than your husband.

The best way to save yourself for marriage is to date someone who is walking the same walk spiritually. Although there will be temptations, if you are both in agreement that you want to abstain from sexual intimacy then you can hold each other accountable. This can also help you decipher quickly whether or not a person who is not on the same page as you should be someone that you should consider dating. Start by adding this to the list of needs versus wants. A man who wants to save himself for marriage should become a **need** and should definitely be on the top of this list.

Dating in the new technology age is not a bad thing as long as you remember to incorporate old fashioned values. Chivalry is not dead. Hold men accountable to treating you the way you deserve to be treated. Set realistic standards. Communicate in ways other than phone, email and text. Face-to-face interaction is always best. Spend time getting to know one another. Don't rush. If he is for you then he will wait for you because he will see your value and know that you are worth the wait. Let the man assume his position as the head. Don't assume the role because you will be out of order. Practice makes perfect so date with the purpose of becoming a wife IF this is your goal. If marriage is not your goal, then know that you shouldn't be sexually intimate either. Scripture backs up everything I've said. If you don't want to take my word for it, then study the Word for yourself. Meditate on it. Live it!

YOU ARE A GOOD THING! That's really what this book boils down to. You are the good thing that will become a good man's help mate. His right hand. His confidant. His friend. His everything. Queens, follow the instructions of the Heavenly Father by *Dating the Christian Way*. This will ensure that your King WILL find you and eventually put a ring on it.

Acknowledgements

TJ Woodard would like to thank:

I would like to thank my Father God for choosing me to endure the things I have for a time as this. For saving me. For trusting me to carry out the purpose that He placed inside of me. For speaking through me. For loving me even when I didn't love myself. I will forever give you all glory and honor.

To my children Lanaiya, DeAndre & DeVonte I love you all with everything that is in me. You all are my greatest accomplishments. Know that I've always wanted the best for you and appreciate all the support and sacrifices you made while I pursued my dreams. Everything I do is for you.

To my mom, my rock, my biggest cheerleader I thank you for always being there for me. Words cannot even express the love I have for you. In your words…I love you more. More for you have shown me what truth faith in God looks like and how to patiently wait for the one God has for me even when I didn't always listen. More for showing me what true strength looks like. More for showing me what true love looks like. I thank you for being there to help me pick up the pieces and rebuild.

To my sisters Gina and Andrae and to my brother Phillip "Antoine" I have learned so much from you all and I admire each one of you for your individual strength and perseverance. I've leaned on you all and you were there for me when it counted the most. I love you.

To my dad, I want you to know that you too have contributed to who I am today. You provide words of encouragement and support and I am forever grateful. I love you.

To my family - my aunts, uncles, cousins, nieces, nephews by blood and by love. Family is truly everything. I am so blessed to have the most supportive family a girl could ever ask for. You all have supported me in many endeavors without judgement. You have loved me though the ups and downs. I love and appreciate each one of you.

To my God Parents - thank you for your continuous love and support. You are my village, always there when I need you. I've learned something from each of you.

To my friends - (you all know who you are) who went into the trenches with me, cried with me, cried for me, prayed for me, prayed with me, supported me, encouraged me and would not let me quit. To the ones who've consistently reminded me that I am a virtuous woman. A woman made by God. A woman who is fearfully and wonderfully made. A Queen.

Last but not least, to my co-author and friend Alton L. Fitch. None of this would be possible without you. You have pushed me beyond my limits and further than I could have ever imagined. Your friendship means the world to me and I am forever grateful to you!

Special Thanks

My Apostle Wayne and Pastor Michelle Green and my Armor of Light Christian Worship Center family – My spiritual leaders and mentors who show true love and support. I love and appreciate you.

Lakesha L. Williams – (Vision to Fruition/Born Overcomers Inc.) Your help with this project goes far beyond words. Your professionalism and willingness to get the job done and get it done right does not go unnoticed. Thank you!

Keisha Robinson – Your help with editing and your support has blessed me tremendously. You roll up your sleeves and jump in and I don't know what I would do without you. I love you sis.

My Partnerships

Minister Missy Jacobs – (Royalty Diadem, Inc.) Words cannot express the love I have for you. We are joined at the hip. We WIN! I love, love, love you!

Nikita Powell – (We Fight Foundation, Inc.) We may not be sisters by blood but definitely sisters by love. I love and appreciate you so much in the short time we've known each other it's like we were friends forever.

Ministers Wendy, LaShelle, & LaShawn – (The Women of Empowerment and Destiny) - My sisters. My prayer warriors and all of my sisters of WOED and Praying Wives of the DMV, you pulled me through. You would not let me go and loved on me when I needed it most. Thank you and I love you!

To all those who I may have missed but have inspired, encouraged, and challenged me in some way, I love and appreciate you much!

Alton L. Fitch would like to thank:

First and foremost I would like to thank Jehovah for allowing me the opportunity to help write this book. Without Him none of this would be possible.

I would also like to thank my mother Lucinda McMillan for raising and making me into the man I have become. She raised three productive children by herself. Both of my siblings have master's degrees, and this was due to her dedication to us.

I would like to acknowledge my two children, Katelyn and Neelen McMillan. They are the most important people in my life and I am extremely grateful and blessed to have such wonderful kids. I love them more than life itself.

I would also like to acknowledge my friends Kevin and Serlea Jones, thank you for everything.

Last but definitely not least, I would like to thank my friend and co-author TJ " Sunshine" Woodard, thank you so much for allowing me to take this journey with you. Words can't express my gratitude.

About the Authors

TJ Woodard

TJ Woodard is a mother, entrepreneur, and a military veteran. She comes from a life of hardships, struggle and knows firsthand how to overcome obstacles. God has had His hand on her life carrying her through each and every situation she has had to endure. Her biggest pride and joy are her three beautiful children Lanaiya, DeAndre and DeVonte and two grandchildren Aiden and Delilah.

TJ is a member of several organizations started by her sister friends and currently leads a program called Queen Series in which she volunteers as a mentor to young women between the ages of 15 - 25 offering advice and education on self-love, self-respect, self-esteem, love and relationships. TJ designed the program after experiencing her own revelation of personal truths following separation from her husband. She recently graduated 11 newly promoted Queens as the first graduating class of the Queen Series program.

TJ's personal experiences have taught her so many things but most importantly how she is an overcomer and how strong she really is. She hopes that her desire to mentor young women in her program as well as her contribution to the We Fight Foundation and Royalty Diadem will show young women that no matter the struggle, no matter the circumstances, not matter what they have been through or are going through that they too can overcome. For their future, the possibilities are endless if they don't quit and keep God first.

One of the things TJ realized and the reason she has made the commitment to help others was that she did not truly understand her worth. Being a Christian and knowing God as her personal Savior, she had not tapped in to her bloodline as the child of the King. She is Royalty. She is a Queen and should be treated as such.

Alton L. Fitch

Alton L Fitch is a father and works as a professional truck driver. He graduated High School in 1989. He currently resides in Baltimore Md. He has a passion for helping young men and women see their true worth and strive for excellence. He has 2 children who are near and dear to his heart and are proud of their accomplishments.

Alton works closely with young men and women encouraging them in areas of finding their true worth and striving for excellence. His passion stems from his childhood, seeing his mom treated in a less desirable way. He recently served as a key contributor working behind the scenes of a mentorship program for young ladies while providing encouragement and assistance where needed.

www.ingramcontent.com/pod-product-compliance
Lightning Source LLC
Chambersburg PA
CBHW070107100426
42743CB00012B/2682